DEDICATION

This book is dedicated to all those whose lives were cut short by COVID-19.

Ar dheis Dé go raibh a n-anam dílis.

Authors: Niamh Hamill and John O' Connell
Editorial Assistance: Tracy Altemus
Art Director/Designer: Lynne DeLade
Photographers: Niamh Hamill, John O' Connell and Aoife Hamill
             (Except where otherwise noted.)
Map Illustrator: Kevin Lowery

All inquiries should be addressed to:
Institute of Study Abroad Ireland
Bundoran, Donegal, Ireland

+353 87 294 1232 (9-5 GMT)
Website: isaireland.com
Email: info@isaireland.com
Skype: irelandstudyabroad

ISBN: 978-1-5272-8728-0

Printed in the United States of America by IngramSpark

FINDING IRELAND
NOTES FROM THE NORTHWEST
BY NIAMH HAMILL AND JOHN O' CONNELL

TABLE OF CONTENTS

INTRODUCTION

A million grassblades, whispering in the breeze
Reminded me I was no one, and the peace
Felt huge inside me, as the night came on.

These lines are taken from a poem by Harry Clifton, titled *A Woman Drives Across Ireland*. For many years now, our business has been to bring visitors across Ireland, to explore, study, learn and enjoy the beautiful and history-soaked landscapes of Donegal and its surrounds. It is what we do, and therefore, when 2020 shut us down, and visitors couldn't come, we decided to adopt the 'Muhammad to the Mountain' approach. If you could not come to the Northwest, then we would bring the Northwest to you.

Ours is a vista of mountains, bogs, lakelands and gnarled, hunchbacked trees. Our coastline is scissor-sharp and wild, with outcrops of islands, stretches of white strands, clumped with seaweeds, starfish, and the here and there footprints of a lone surfer. There are traditions of separations and partings, islanders leaving the islands, countryfolk leaving for cities, city folk leaving for foreign shores, borders, checkpoints, Gaelgóirí, Béarlóirí, Protestants, Catholics, bad roads, mad roads—as the slogan goes, it's different up here. But despite the chequered history and many misfortunes endured in this part of Ireland, we have never heard a Donegal man or woman say a disparaging word about the landscape. The ravaged, rough beauty is the backdrop to our lives, the crashing Atlantic is the pulse in our veins.

The landscapes and seascapes of the Northwest are not just wild and wonderful, they are keepers of a rich, magical history. Like our boglands, they are layered, palimpsests of the experiences of Stone Age farmers, Bronze Age metalworkers, high kings and queens, monks, Vikings, Normans, Planters, Gentry, Mothers, Farmers, fiddle players, tattie hoakers, screamers, showbands and surfers. Our history, culture and scenery are the best resources we have here. That, and a welcome for everyone.

So, as 2020 sabre-rattled at us, and every flick of a switch brought sadness and fear, we decided we would share our wild and wonderful world. Beginning on March 18, 2020, we chose a different location each day, somewhere in the Northwest, and through the magic of social media, we shared each walk with hundreds of our friends. We continued this project through summer, fall and winter, and now we are bringing some of those best days to you here. Throughout all of the craziness of 2020, including lockdowns, furloughs, circuit breakers, protest marches and presidential campaigns, we took refuge in the astonishing beauty of our landscapes and seascapes, and the enduring sense of stoicism and courage that seems to prevail in Ireland's Northwest. We did our best to communicate the beauty, history, mythology and magic of this gorgeous corner of Ireland, with the hope that it would do for you what it does for us, and what the poem above suggests—humble us, restore us, and replace our anxieties with a huge peace.

Enjoy,
Niamh & John

CARVING A LANDSCAPE

IRELAND'S CURRENT LANDSCAPE WAS sculpted by the last Ice Age, which ended about 12,000 years ago. As the ice melted, new valleys, rivers and lakes were created by the moving glaciers, and left us with the landscape we see today. Although it is very scenic, parts of the Northwest, especially Donegal, are agriculturally poor. Our corner of Ireland is characterised by boglands, lakelands, dramatic coastlines, tough hard mountains glittering with quartzite to the north and tightly packed hills known as drumlins to the southeast. County Leitrim is famous for its glens; Sligo for its Dartry Mountains, especially the iconic flat-topped Ben Bulben; Fermanagh for the lakelands; Cavan for its unique karstic burren. Donegal, the largest of these counties, and the one with the most coastline, has all of the above elements with the added bonus of spectacular coastal cliffs, numerous sandy coves, beaches and off-shore islands.

From the arrival of the first farmers to the present day, it is impossible to think about the cultural, social, political and economic development of Ireland without an understanding that the landscape (and climate) is everything. The glaciers provided our ancients with the stone to build their primitive cathedrals. The rivers provided a water transport network for our early

<<<

Erris, (Iar Ros, meaning western headland), in County Mayo, has one of the loveliest loop walks in the Northwest. Rock formations over a billion years old are found along the rugged coastline.

Tory Island, (Oileán Thoraí, Island of outlaws), nine miles off the coast of Donegal, has many stunning geological features, almost all of which have been incorporated into fabulous myths and legends.

Christian monastic sites, Viking towns and Norman castles. Subsequent invaders would take the better land and abandon the bogs and hills. Like many other countries, the indigent were corralled to the poorest real estate. The Irish Language would also be relegated to certain spaces. In the Northwest, artificial political borders would create huge difficulties for people who had been neighbours for generations.

The work of the last Ice Age carved out an island canvas upon which generations of people would make their mark. Most people would come from other places in the world, constantly reinventing ways in which they would shape the landscape, but ultimately, this boggy, misty, sun-dappled, furious and watery world would have the same effect on those who would stay long enough—it would lure, seduce and leak into the soul until you could not forget it.

Ballintra (Baile an tSrath, meaning townland along a river), in County Donegal, is a limestone-based area of gentle rolling hills called drumlins, peppered with small lakes and winding country roads.

The Dartry Mountains are a distinctive feature of Counties Leitrim and Sligo. During the last Ice Age, back-to-back glaciers carved the limestone Dartry plateau into a stunning landscape of sculpted mountains and valleys.

Beltra (Beal Trá, meaning 'mouth of the beach'),
overlooking Knocknarea, County Sligo. Many Irish
mountain ranges hug the Atlantic, creating dramatic
vistas of sheer drops down to the sea.

Donegal is home to one of the most incredible features of the Wild Atlantic Way, the sea cliffs at Sliabh Liag—best appreciated by boat trip. Note the Napoleonic watchtower on top.

ANCIENT IRELAND

IT IS DIFFICULT TO COMPREHEND HOW much ancient history is dotted around our landscape. If you witness the crowds who visit the Pyramids, or Athenian Temples, you realise what a privilege it is to have our own ancient temples and sacred spaces scattered around the countryside, accessible and usually free to explore. Our ancients had little to work with —great boulders dropped by the glaciers and a forested landscape. With primitive tools and truly amazing engineering skills, they built monuments of all sizes, many still standing today.

Every Irish schoolchild quickly becomes familiar with the terms passage grave, cairn and dolmen, not just because they are popular destinations for the annual school fieldtrip, but also because these structures are so old, mysterious and magical. Constructed during the Neolithic period in Ireland, around 4000–2500 BC, there are over 1600 of these tombs. While some of the more impressive monuments have been incorporated into carefully managed heritage sites, many more are to be found in random fields, atop mountains or nestled in among the forests.

We do not know the purpose of these monuments. Many were aligned with the rising or setting sun at equinox or solstice and feature beautiful carved patterns of spirals and curves. Many have revealed cremated or unburnt remains, so it is likely they were

<<<

The Kilclooney Dolmen in County Donegal is a Neolithic monument which dates to between 4,000 to 3,000 BC. Dolmens, or portal tombs created sacred spaces to commemorate the dead.

The Cairn Dolmen at Cavan Burren Park.

important centres of ritual and very connected to the natural phenomena that were central to the existence of these early Irish inhabitants. It is impossible to visit these places and not marvel at the skill with which their construction was executed. These sites were also very influential on later generations, who put these places at the centre of their myths and stories.

The ancients chose the locations of their sacred spaces with such attention to detail that they frequently were repurposed, as sites for stone circles in the Bronze Age, monastic sites in the early Christian era, and sites for forts and castles as later civilisations were established. This was probably for both logistical and symbolic reasons, but you will often find that at every heritage site, there will be archaeological remnants from several periods of Irish history.

These standing stones are part of an Iron Age stone circle at Beltany, County Donegal.

A small cairn in the townland of Drumskinny, (from Droim Scine meaning knife ridge), in County Fermanagh. The cairn is adjacent to a stone circle, and also appears to be part of a larger network of megaliths in the area.

Deerpark, County Sligo. This arrangement of stone is known as a court cairn. Almost all of the court cairns in Ireland are in the northern half of the country.

This prehistoric decoration is known as Atlantic rock art. Cup, ring and rosette motifs are carved onto this boulder in the Cavan Burren.

An old graveyard in County Fermanagh is home to this incredible two-sided idol, known as 'The Janus Figure.' One side is male, the other is female, and is most likely an Iron Age invocation of fertility.

Myths and Magic

THERE IS MUCH ABOUT OUR ANCIENT people we do not know, as for many centuries nothing was written down in any form we could understand. It was not until the first missionaries began to arrive in the 5th century that they began to record the fabulous tales and stories that were told and retold by the 'file' (pronounced fill-ah) or poet. However, it is worth noting that those who had documented the old stories were not without an agenda, they were invested in changing the belief system of the pagan Irish. Therefore, it is not surprising that many of the tales end with baptism, the appearance of saints and redemptive Christian ritual. Thankfully, however, the more magical and fantastic elements of Gaelic mythology were not rendered invisible by this evangelistic perspective. In fact, they are embodied, not just in the narratives, but artistically in many of the beautifully illustrated manuscripts from that time.

The preservation of Irish mythology was further secured because much of it was written in the vernacular, and against high odds, the Irish language survived. Scholars have been able to translate and study the old stories, ensuring their viability and their utility in providing sources of magical fantasy for new interpretations. The survival of the Irish language has also preserved within it a folk memory that dates back to pre-Christian times.

<<<

Lough Gill, (Loch Gile, meaning bright lake) nestles between the counties of Leitrim and Sligo. Lough Gill abounds in mythology and inspired much of the work of Irish poet W.B. Yeats.

Niamh and John at the Giant's Causeway in County Antrim. According to Irish mythology, the causeway was built between Ireland and Scotland by Irish hero Finn McCool (Fionn Mac Cumhaill).

Irish mythology has some very well-known characters and stories, wonderfully and indelibly associated with particular places and placenames. It is almost impossible to go anywhere in Ireland without a reference to mythology—The Giant's Causeway, Diarmuid and Gráinne's Cave or Erris, the final destination of the Children of Lir. Almost every geographical feature has an association with a story, and frequently, there will be an Irish placename that secures this connection. This means that almost everywhere you wander, there is a mythical dimension to the landscape that doubles the pleasure of your visit.

Balor's Fort, on Tory Island was supposedly the home of Balor of the Evil Eye, a terrifying, mythical cyclops who imprisoned his own daughter, and was finally slain by his grandson, Lugh.

The extraordinary scenery at Malin Head, County Donegal was the setting for the Jedi Planet Ahch-To in the most recent *Star Wars* movies.

Oakfield Park, Donegal. *The Children of Lir* is a well-known tale about a paternal king and his unfortunate children, Fionnuala, Aodh, Conn and Fiachra, who were changed into swans by their evil stepmother, Aoife.

Pollnagollum Cave in County Fermanagh was used to film Beric Dondarrion's hideout in season 3 of the TV series *Game of Thrones*.

This Cairn at the top of Knocknarea Mountain is believed to be the resting place of Queen Maeve of Connacht. Legend says she was buried in a standing position to face her enemies in Ulster.

THE FAIRY FOLK

FAIRY FOLKLORE IS PART OF IRISH

mythology, but it is also part of a larger narrative in Irish culture. Its survival and endurance through many cultural transitions is a testament to the functionality of folklore within a community. One of the oldest origin myths of Irish culture is the story of the Tuatha De Dannan, an ancient race of people with supernatural powers. After a battle with their arch enemies, the Milesians, they chose to occupy the underworld, and took to the sidhe (mounds) and became known as the Sídhe (pronounced 'shee'). The word banshee is formed from two Irish words, 'bean' meaning woman, and the Sídhe.

It is interesting that the Sídhe were not demonised by the Christian scribes who would later rework fairy tales, and they remained in the cultural psyche as karmic elements who would reward the good and punish the bad. The fairies would enjoy a further reincarnation in Anglo-Irish literature when they captured the imagination of writers such as W.B. Yeats, William Allingham, and Augusta Gregory. Fairy folklore was now present in two languages, and in the oral and literary tradition.

Many fairy stories are allegorical. The concept of the changeling, for example, reflected parental anxieties about infant disorders or abnormalities. Unexplained phenomenon were simply attributed

<<<

Tullan Strand, Bundoran, is one of the finest stretches of golden sand in Donegal. Rainbows are a daily event during winter.

Homemade fairy doors are a common sight around the forests, often made by local children as a school project.

to the work of the fairies, worked around an ethical code that also served as a kind of moral compass, particularly for children. Much of the folklore is concerned with preserving nature; a lot of bad luck is associated with disrupting trees, hills or rivers where fairies live. It seems that an indigenous knowledge of the importance of the ecosystems permeated folklore, and we are certain that many beautiful places in Ireland remained undisturbed simply because of fear of fairy revenge.

The only fairy-figure that became corrupted over time is the leprechaun. Originally supposed to be a mischievous cobbler-fairy, its form was re-imagined by cartoonists based on derogatory 19th century caricatures of the Irish. It has no place in any authentic representation of Irish culture. While you will see many leprechauns in the gift shops of Ireland, they are almost solely for tourist consumption.

The Fairy Bridges in Bundoran are beautiful ridges of stone over a steep drop to the Atlantic. On stormy days, the churning ocean blows sea spray up around the bridges, creating an ethereal atmosphere.

Sídhe, or fairy folk, were often believed to live amongst the plentiful and colourful fungi of the undergrowth. Did they make the mushrooms magic?

It is considered very bad luck to disturb paths, forts or trees that are associated with fairy folklore. Still today, people prefer to leave such places undisturbed. Just in case.

Glencar Waterfall is the location of W.B. Yeats' famous fairy poem, *The Stolen Child. (Photo by Todd Vorenkamp)*

Fungi are present in a multiplicity of fairy folklore, and in folk remedies and rituals.

The Cave of the Cats in County Roscommon, was believed to be an entrance to either the Gates of Hell, or Tír na nÓg (Land of Eternal Youth).

THE MONASTERIES

CONTRARY TO POPULAR OPINION,

Ireland was not single-handedly converted from pagan to Christian by St. Patrick, but Patrick did exist, and the written history of Ireland begins with him. Two of his manuscripts have survived, so you can actually read the story of Patrick in his own words, but you may be disappointed to find no mention of snakes or shamrocks. These, and many other legends about Patrick would be invented later to lend credibility or celebrity to various locations all around Ireland.

Christianity came to Ireland in the 5th century, and with it came literacy, which had a huge cultural impact. By the 12th century, there was a very significant infrastructure of monastic sites, including large ecclesiastical sites like Clonmacnoise and Glendalough. The bigger churches had A-list saints like Brigid and Colm, but there were many small churches founded by local missionaries. All around Ireland, there are churches dedicated to saints you have never heard of, such as Assicus, Molaise and Tigernach. It was also quite the trend to find the most isolated and inhospitable places to establish churches, and you can find evidence of this in many remote places, particularly on offshore islands.

Over time, the monasteries became responsible for the education and healthcare of the community, and many of them also grew

<<<

The Killaghtee Church Ruins in Donegal are a very inconspicuous home to the extraordinary 7th-century cross of Aedh.

This beautiful sculpture of the Four Masters by James McKenna is by the Drowse River in Leitrim.

extremely wealthy and powerful. Their power would survive the Viking and Norman invasions, and some would even survive Henry VIII's dissolution orders, but by the 17th century, all of these sites were closed, and many were burnt or destroyed.

Ironically, the threat to the monasteries prompted some very inspired record-keeping for fear that the early Christian history of Ireland would be completely wiped out. One of the best examples of this is *The Annals of the Four Masters*, which was compiled in the Northwest of Ireland. Written in Irish, the Annals were originally commissioned to record the names of the many Irish saints. Great foresight by the four compilers led them to collect vast material from all over Ireland, including records of pre-Christian mythology, manuscripts, diaries, records and original contributions by the four authors themselves.

Tullyaughnish church, in Ramelton, County Donegal, is an interesting example of a seventeenth century Protestant Church which incorporated elements of 12th century monastic design.

Cong Abbey, County Mayo, became an Augustinian Abbey under High King Turlough O'Connor in the 12th century. The ruins are a wonderful example of early medieval ecclesiastical architecture.

Ballysaggart, (from Baile an tSagairt, meaning townland of the priest), is a scenic area at St. John's Point, County Donegal, with the ruin of a medieval Franciscan abbey overlooking the pier.

The Killaghtee Cross, which dates from around 650 AD. It pre-dates the high crosses, and you can still make out the Maltese cross carved into the slab.

Gateway to the monk's fishing house at Cong Abbey, County Mayo.

Irish Castles

IRISH CASTLES ARE PROBABLY ONE

of the most popular sites for visitors, and we are fortunate to have so many, particularly in the Northwest. It was the Norman invasion that introduced the stone-built tower-house to Ireland, and Irish chieftains quickly realized the benefits of such impenetrable strongholds for their own security. Early castles were built solely for defence and are usually quite simple in terms of design —a stone 'bawn' or tower house surrounded by a high stone wall. The location of a castle was extremely important. Access to a waterway was crucial, as was an elevated position. As these strategic requirements would have also applied to earlier settlements, many castles were built on former sites, and this is why we often find evidence of different periods of history in the same place. It is also why Irish castles tend to be very scenic with locations on high ground, beside a river, or along the coast.

One common feature of the Irish castle is that it would have had an Irish name and an English name associated with it. When Ireland was colonized in the 17th century, almost all of the land was confiscated from the powerful Gaelic families and redistributed to English and Scottish nobles. The new British owners were encouraged to knock down vernacular buildings and rebuild in a more English style, but thankfully, most of them

<<<

Doe Castle sits on the shore of Sheephaven Bay, County Donegal. It was home to the MacSweeneys, and also has its very own legend of star-crossed lovers, Aileen and Turlough.

Donegal Castle was the seat of power of the great Red Hugh O'Donnell. After the Plantation of Ulster, it became the home of the Brooke Family. Now beautifully restored by the Office of Public Works.

did not. Some of these new owners did not survive, and had their castles burnt or destroyed. Some of the more successful owners added new castles to their estates, or simply added on modifications or extensions.

By the 18th century, the Anglo-Irish landlord wanted something more salubrious than a tower-house, and what would become known as the 'big house' appeared on the landscapes. Ironically, the stone castles introduced by the Normans were terribly impractical for domestic purposes—they were very hard to heat, furnish or decorate, and few remained inhabited. Some of the grander castles were redeveloped as luxury hotels, many more have been rescued by the Office of Public Works. Some still languish as ruins, ivy-covered and crow-murdered, their stonework a silent witness to many forgotten battles and bloodshed.

Castle Caldwell, in County Fermanagh, was built during the Plantation of Ulster. The Caldwell family would later make their fortune from the discovery of china clay on their property, now known worldwide as Belleek Pottery.

One of the most beautifully restored castles in Ireland is the former home of the O'Rourkes, on the shore of Lough Gill. Now known as Parkes Castle, it overlooks Lough Gill and Yeats' beloved Lake Isle of Innisfree.

MacSwyne Castle ruins at St. John's Point, County Donegal.

Dunluce Castle, in County Antrim was home to the McQuillans, the MacDonalds, and its very own Banshee (alledgedly).
(Photo by Lynne DeLade)

Castle McGrath, in Donegal, is a remnant of the powerful McGrath dynasty, which included the notorious Myler McGrath. Myler fought with just about everyone he knew, but lived to be 100, so he wins.

AN GORTA MÓR-THE GREAT HUNGER

THE GREAT HUNGER OF 1845-1850 IS
sometimes called the Potato Famine, but it really had nothing to do with famine. There was plenty of food available in Ireland during these years, and yet over a million people died of starvation, and another million became migrants. In truth, the Great Hunger was the catastrophic result of British administrative policies, beginning in the 16th century, when laws were enacted that characterised the poor as a dependent section of society that were lazy and threatening, and had to be controlled.

The best illustration of this point is the construction of the workhouse in Irish towns in the early 19th century. By then, the population of Ireland was over six million, and at least a third of this number were close to starvation. Destitution was widespread, but the British government failed again and again to address the situation. Ultimately, their solution was to introduce the workhouse system to Ireland, despite evidence that it would not solve the root causes of wide scale poverty.

George Wilkinson, an English architect, was hired to design a template for the Irish workhouse. He received only two-thirds of the budget that was allocated to English workhouses. Construction began in 1839 with three work house options;

<<<

A mass famine grave at Ballyshannon, County Donegal. The bodies of at least 800 workhouse inmates were buried here during the famine. No records exist of these people.

In 1995 the Donegal Association of New York funded a memorial plaque at the Ballyshannon graveyard.

small, medium and large. The Poor Law Commissioners ordered that 'the style of the building is intended to be of the cheapest description compatible with durability.' Explicit instructions were given that the workhouse must offer less comfort than any other solution. Relief was only given if the whole family entered the workhouse, but families were immediately segregated on arrival.

Because the root causes of Irish poverty were never addressed, catastrophe was inevitable. The only escape route from death by starvation or disease was emigration. Since the Great Hunger, little has changed in discourses of poverty and migration. Ireland is no longer poor or hungry, but many other nations are. They try to emigrate as the Irish once did, but sadly migrants are unwelcome in many western countries now.

The Workhouse at Ballyshannon, County Donegal.

Historic Ballyshannon

THE WORKHOUSE

BUILT IN 1842 TO CATER FOR THE POOR OF THE AREA. AT THE HEIGHT OF THE FAMINE IT HOUSED 900 PEOPLE.

COMHAIRLE BAILE BHÉAL ÁTHA SEANAIDH

TEACH NA mBOCHT

THE WORKHOUSE

BALLYSHANNON TOWN COUNCIL

Famine Pot
The Famine Pot used in the Ballyshannon Workhouse
Donated by Ignatius Lysaght, Ballyshannon

MARY ANN AND ...AH McDERMOTT

SALLY LENNON

The Mall Quay, Ballyshannon, County Donegal. Ballyshannon was not a major emigrant port, but several ships did depart to Canada and America during famine times.

Derelict cottages are a common feature of the Northwest, testaments to widescale eviction, emigration and death.

This sculpture by Niall Bruton commemorates the 30,000 people that emigrated from Sligo Harbour between 1847 and 1851.

the wild atlantic way

the coastline of the northwest

has beguiled visitors for centuries. Now known as the Wild Atlantic Way, its craggy, gnarled coastline with its cliffs and sea-stacks, offshore islands and magnificent stretches of sandy beach, is perhaps the most impressive feature of this part of Ireland. There are 3,000 miles of energetic Atlantic Ocean between the Northwest coast and Canada, the nearest western neighbour. However, Ireland is warmer than other areas at the same latitude on the other side of the Ocean, because of the North Atlantic Current and the Gulf Stream. The dominant influence on Ireland's climate is the Atlantic Ocean, and it has also been the dominant influence on the culture of this part of Ireland, past and present.

Atlantic weather brings rain and wind at unexpected angles, and varying degrees of light and shade. There's a difference between a soft day, which is one of mist, gentle rainfall and low sky, and an Atlantic storm, whipping up clouds, waves and erasing the horizon in a green-grey fury. And then there are the blue-sky days, when high pressure hovers overhead, and suddenly the ocean becomes majestic in its glittering beauty, silver light dancing on the wavelets. It is entirely possible to experience each of these weather variations in any given week and any given season.

<<<

Murder Hole Beach, County Donegal.

Limpets are extraordinary creatures. They move around in seawater, but return to the exact same spot on their rock during low tide.

The Atlantic has been our source of food, industry, tourism and recreation, and significantly, our escape route many times when the going got tough. It was not just the fishing boats that kept communities going during hard times, but all too often, the emigrant ships taking generations of Irish people to all corners of the globe. The Wild Atlantic Way has been both treacherous and generous, and in recent years, the coastal route along the Northwest has become a very popular drive for visitors to Ireland.

There is no good or bad time of year to visit the Wild Atlantic Way. It is majestic in calm, in storm and in flux. It is present in Irish history, legend, mythology and folklore. And it's waiting here for you, all year round.

The Lighthouse at St. John's Point, County Donegal.

A summer sunset swim on a Donegal beach should be on everyone's bucket list.

Sea Thrift is a pretty pink wildflower which grows profusely on cliffs, rocks and along the shoreline from April to July.

The clear waters along Bundoran's West End were visited for their restorative properties from the early 19th century onwards.

The very pretty Mermaids Cove, near Mullaghmore, County Sligo.

WILD IRELAND COAST

NOTHING IS AS UPLIFTING FOR THE

soul as a walk along the beaches of Donegal. Donegal has more coastline than any other county in Ireland, and it has two main characteristics—rocky cliff edges, and long stretches of white sandy beach. Even at the height of the busy seasons, it is possible to have a beach to yourself, some rock pools to explore, a promontory of barnacled foreland to cast a line or a mysterious cave to investigate. Wildflowers thrive, and there are few sights as glorious as the clusters of pink sea thrift clinging to the cliff edges of the wild Atlantic.

Donegal has no shortage of providers who will bring you kayaking, fishing, whale or shark watching, diving or coasteering. Surfing is extremely popular, because of the consistency of waves all year round. The air is fresh and bracing. The sand, varying in colours from deep golden to powder white, is soft and clean. There are also large areas of shingle, with an incredible array of pebbles of all colours and types, sanded to smooth spheres by the constant rolling sea. Jutting rock interrupts the coves, draped in multi-coloured seaweeds and sea creatures. Burgundy anemones, fluorescent green spirulina and leathery kelps hide a wealth of small sea life, including whelks, crabs, gobies, sea urchins and starfish. Cracks and crevices are stuffed with clusters of mussels, periwinkles and limpets.

<<< ————————————————————————

Carrickfin Beach, with Gola Island in the distance (right). Gola is featured in the traditional Irish song Báidín Fheilimí *(Feilim's little boat).*

The Atlantic coast has many interesting caves and chambers, perfect for aspiring pirates. Murder Hole Beach, Donegal.

One of the interesting developments here in Donegal is sustainable seaweed harvesting. It has become fashionable to use seaweeds in cosmetic products, foodstuffs, and health supplements. But locals here will remind you that this was a common practice in years gone by. Seaweed was gathered in bundles and carted home by donkeys, to be spread as fertilizer on vegetable plots. Seaweeds were also collected and dried for use in the kitchen, and provided both nutrition and flavor to a sparse coastal diet.

There are many customs, superstitions, traditions and folklore associated with life on the shore. With such a diverse and colourful environment, one can easily imagine why mermaids, selkie, sunken otherworlds, and monsters beyond the shallows are all part of the imagination of the coastal folklore.

Tidal pools make for great shore safaris for younger (or older) coastal explorers.

Mullaghmore, County Sligo. The kayakers are safe and well, enjoying a well-earned beer in the Pier Head Hotel!

WILD IRELAND HEDGEROWS

ONE OF THE GREAT PLEASURES OF
roaming the Donegal countryside is the abundance of hedgerows which border the roadsides and small fields, and reclaim derelict homesteads. Each season offers a distinctive palette of colour. Springtime is a burst of yellow, with butterscotch gorse spiking skywards, while lemony clutches of primroses and wild golden daffodils scatter the ditches. Early April fills the forest floors with bluebells, and summer explodes in pinks and purples, with the dramatic swagger of the foxgloves competing with bright-eyed daisies, the elegant fuchsia and rampant bubble-gum heathers. Autumn whirls in, with her confetti of yellow and orange leaves, and buffet of blackberries, and winter gifts us the Christmassy greens and reds of hollies and ivies.

There is no part of Ireland that is without hedgerows, and although some date back as far as the 8th century, most of them were planted in the 18th century. They are all man-made. Farmers deliberately planted boundaries of thorny bushes to fence in cattle and sheep, and these became dense sanctuaries for wildlife, supporting species such as badgers, owls, hedgehogs, stoats, blackbirds and innumerable plants, birds, butterflies and other insects. Hedgerows now provide a home for most Irish wildlife, and it is imperative that they are preserved. They sustain wildlife diversity and are also vital in

<<< ————————————————————————

A number of walking trails have been developed along the old train routes of Donegal. This is the old Donegal-Killybegs line.

The bees love the hawthorn flowers, which which dazzle the Irish country-side throughout the months of May and June.

providing food and shelter for pollinators, cleaning our air, storing carbon and act as a defense against flooding.

Wildlife legislation in Ireland forbids the cutting back of hedgerows between March and August each year, primarily to protect nesting birds, but all of the wildlife benefits from this law. It means that there is a wonderful lushness and verdancy along the roadsides and pathways during these months. There is a vast network of small, barely used roadways that have now been developed as trails, and they make for a joyous ramble all around the Northwest, never too far from a delicious pot of tea and homemade scone, or a refreshing pint.

If there is one small benefit from our 2020 lockdown, it has been a revived appreciation for the cornucopian margins of our country roads and their bountiful hedgerows.

Blackthorn bushes are hardy native bushes, their white flowers heralding the arrival of spring, their sloe fruits heralding a nice autumn gin!

Blatantly disobeying social distancing rules, August 2020.

The hardy fuschia is known in some parts of
the Northwest as *Deora Dé*, God's teardrops.

WILD IRELAND FORESTS

THE FIRST HUMANS ARRIVED IN

Ireland about 9,000 years ago, and were met with a forested island, covered in oak and elm, birch, willow and Scots pine trees. Animals that are now extinct, such as bears and wolves, made their home in these forests, so the earliest people kept to the coast, rivers and upland hill tops. From about 4000 BC, the woodlands were disrupted by our first farmers, but their impact was low, with forests either regrowing, or developing into boglands. It was not until the middle of the 16th century that there was a serious clearance of native forestry, and this, of course, coincides with colonization and plantation. Wood was cut down for ship building, cooperage, furnaces, and for export. Many of the new planters cleared land for pasture and tillage.

Sadly, by the beginning of the 19th century, almost all of Ireland's forests were depleted. With them, many native animals disappeared, including wolves, bears, wild boars and the red squirrel. There was a brief respite in the middle of the 18th century when it became fashionable for wealthy landowners to have private demesnes. However, during the famine years of the 19th century, landlord bankruptcy and new tenant laws saw the woodlands once again cut down and cleared.

<<< ——————————————————

Few sights are as lovely as the discovery of a bluebell-carpeted forest in April.

Fungi play an important role in the breakdown of dead wood.

Today, about 11% of the Republic of Ireland is afforested, and about half of these forests are state-owned and managed. More attention is now being paid to the conservation of forests, boglands and coastlines. Stricter environmental controls have been applied concerning the protection of water quality, biodiversity, harvesting, landscape and archaeology. The counties of the Northwest; Donegal, Leitrim, Sligo and Cavan; have about 125,000 hectares of woodland, many of which have been developed as public trails. Many of our lockdown walks were through these beautiful forest hikes, and it is a joy to witness the sheer variety and vibrancy of forest life, from the ferns, fungi and foxgloves on the forest floor, to the woody vines that entwine themselves around a great variety of trees, including conifers, yew, Scots pine, oak, ash, birch, hazel and alder.

Ardnamona Forest Walk, Lough Eske, County Donegal.

Knader Forest, Ballyshannon, County Donegal.

Autumn in Deerpark Forest, Calry, County Sligo.

Cavan Burren Park, County Cavan.

Lough Navar Forest, County Fermanagh.

WILD IRELAND BOGLANDS

BOGLANDS ARE A VERY FAMILIAR

feature in Donegal, and for a long time they were mainly used as a source of fuel. Boglands are formed from peat, a type of soil that is poor in nutrients and therefore of little value to the farmer. Bogs form where there is a lot of rain, and the combination of semi-decomposing vegetation and water creates layers of a soft, wet, spongy ground cover that grows slowly over time. The word 'bog' comes from the Gaelic word for 'soft,' and the layered bogs of Ireland have turned out many artefacts and treasures from Ireland's past, including preserved bog bodies.

Until very recently, boglands were considered agriculturally worthless, and it was the poorer people of the Western seaboard who found themselves relocated to these areas. They were forced to find ways of either reclaiming the bogs where they could, or cutting layers of wet peat from the mountain, drying it over the summer and burning it as fuel during the winter. The scent of a turf fire is characteristic of a visit to Donegal, as is the view of miles of unfenced, waterlogged, yellowish-brown mountainside, interrupted now and then by bursts of heather and hardy sheep.

Cutting and saving the turf was an essential part of living on the Atlantic coast, and the turf fire was one of the most important features of the old Irish homestead. Despite severe poverty in many of these regions, having access to fuel for heat and for cooking was a blessing for many families. Even the

<<<

Bog lake at Mullaghduff, County Donegal.

The cleverly camouflaged bog frog.

smallest of cottages had large hearths with an iron hook over the open fire that boiled water, baked bread and cooked the potatoes. Before machinery became available, it was the sturdy donkey that was burdened with baskets or creadles to carry the turf from the bog to the homestead.

Recently, however, there has been a concerted effort by environmentalists to conserve the boglands and to cease the traditional practice of turfcutting. Bogs are significant habitats, and they are also very important for flood control and carbon storage. A lot of damage has been done to the Atlantic bogs, and conservationists are begging government agencies to act before it is too late and the bogs disappear forever. The bog is tricky for the hiker to navigate—you will inevitably fall or get sucked into a swampy hole at some stage, but it also is a joy to witness this unkempt, ancient place with its speckled birds, camouflaged frogs, wild grasses and heathers.

The Barnesmore Gap, County Donegal.

Sheep are hardy animals, suited to the inhospitable landscapes of the Wild Atlantic Way.

Donkeys were important working animals in the Northwest but are now mostly kept as pets.

It's no wonder Irish yarn keeps you warm. It's been well-tested!

Cottongrass, or bog cotton is a common feature of the boglands.

A hand-cut turf bank, Ardcrone, County Donegal.

BEAUTIFUL BUNDORAN

UNLIKE MANY OTHER IRISH TOWNS,

Bundoran's genesis was as a beautiful and recuperative summer resort, initiated by the Viscount of Enniskillen, who built himself Bundoran's first holiday home in 1777. He was emulated by other ascendancy families, who found the brisk sea air and natural cliff promenades of the West End restorative and scenic. Local families provided the necessary services and produce for the tourists, and such has been the nature of the town ever since.

The arrival of the railway in 1866 had a huge economic and cultural impact on the area, allowing people from all over Ireland to vacation by the ocean. Tourism continued to grow, and thousands of people would visit during the summer season, flocking the beaches by day and the dance halls by night. Venues such as the famous Astoria Ballroom were open seven nights a week, and Bundoran became very well-known for its calibre of great local musicians and bands. Regular cabaret nights and drama productions proved extremely popular and added to Bundoran's reputation for fun.

It was, of course, the proximity of the Atlantic Ocean that was always the main attraction, providing sound, sight and salty air as the backdrop to everything. It was no surprise that the sport of surfing would find a home in a community so connected to the

<<<

A summer sunset from 'The View,' Bundoran's magnificent ferris wheel.

Bundoran's seaside amusements have been a highlight for family vacations for generations.

sea. By the late '80s, Bundoran had a reputation as one of the best surf destinations in the world.

Donegal has been rediscovered once more by international visitors who are not just enamoured by the history, culture and the scenery, but by the famous friendly welcome that Donegal has for people of all creed, colour and kin. Donegal is a home away from home, and there is a warm welcome here for allcomers that you will find intoxicating and irresistible.

As you can see from the photographs in this book, Bundoran and its surrounds are beautiful any time of year. We will be waiting to show you around our neighbourhood in person when you are ready to make the trip. We look forward to your visit.

Bundoran by night. *(Photo by Clint Saunders)*

Photo credits: Johnny Gallagher by Eugene T. Hamill, Surfboards and Rainbow by Todd Vorenkamp, Sunset by Clint Saunders. Opposite page, Lynne DeLade.

Snow on the gorse bushes at the Barnesmore Gap, Donegal.